Great Queens and Kings of th

About the Images (Clockwise from top left): *Queen Tiye of Kemet, Emperor Menelik II of Ethiopia, Queen Nzinga of Ndongo and Matamba, and The Pyramids of Meroë (Capital City of the once great kingdom of Kush).*

Teach + Heal + Build

Teach people about their real history so they can find their strength. Knowing about yourself is an important way to understand the world and learn new things in school.

Heal from the hurt of hatred, being left out, and wrong information. People who go through this can learn who they are and become stronger in making their own choices.

Build strong and happy communities after learning about yourself and healing from hurt caused by hatred.

Teaching people about their true history helps them find their strengths. Knowing about the past helps people understand where they fit in the world and feel confident in learning. Learning about history also helps people feel proud of who they are and think more clearly. It's not just schoolwork, but a way to grow and think.

Healing from the pain of hatred and being left out is important for growth. When people heal, they can learn to believe in themselves and make their own choices. With this knowledge and healing, people can help build strong and happy communities.

Brian Knowles

Author and Founder of Power Builders, LLC

> " *A people without knowledge of their past history, origin, and culture is like a tree without roots.* "
>
> **Marcus Garvey**

BOLDLY BLACK:
Afrocentric History Workbook Series
Volume 2: Great Queens and Kings of the African Continent
Teacher's Manual

The Pan-African flag, also called the Red, Black, and Green flag, was created in 1920 by Marcus Garvey and the Universal Negro Improvement Association (UNIA). It stands for unity and freedom for people of African heritage all over the world. The red represents the struggle for freedom, the black stands for African people, and the green shows the land's richness and hope for the future. This flag is a symbol of pride, strength, and togetherness for African people everywhere.

5 Essential Tips for Teaching Black History

1. **Emphasize the Fullness of the Experience:** While acknowledging the struggles, also celebrate the resilience, creativity, and joy that have defined African and African American histories. Highlight achievements in art, music, science, literature, and community building.

2. **Avoid Stereotypes:** Be mindful not to reduce African or African American experiences solely to what is portrayed in the media and avoid interpreting their values and norms through a Eurocentric lens.

3. **Celebrate African Cultural Contributions**: Introduce students to the richness and diversity of African cultures prior to the transatlantic slave trade, highlighting their significant contributions to the arts and sciences.

4. **Acknowledge the Diversity of the African Diasporic Experience:** Highlight the varied experiences within the African Diasporic community, including different regional, ethnic, class, gender, and religious perspectives, to avoid one-dimensional portrayals.

5. **Encourage Critical Thinking:** Ask students to critically engage with historical events and figures, considering both the challenges and the strategies people used to overcome them, and how these moments shaped American society.

Image generated using AI

Scope and Sequence

Content Overview

Royalty on the African continent has a rich and diverse history, with monarchs playing key roles in shaping the culture, politics, and social structures of various kingdoms and empires. From the powerful pharaohs of ancient Egypt to the revered queens and kings of Mali, and Kush. African royalty has been marked by leadership, wisdom, and resilience. These rulers were not only political leaders but also spiritual guides, military strategists, and cultural icons.

Topic:

Great Queens and Kings of the African Continent

Suggested Time:
2 –3 Weeks

Essential Questions:

How did African royalty influence the culture, politics, and social structures of their kingdoms and empires?

Learning Objectives:

Students will be able to identify and describe the roles and contributions of African monarchs, explaining their impact on culture, politics, and society in various historical kingdoms and empires.

Reading and writing standards:

- Explain events, procedures, ideas, or concepts in a historical text, including what happened and why, based on specific information in the text.

- Quote accurately from a text when explaining what the text says explicitly and when drawing inferences from it.

- Write informative/explanatory texts to examine a topic and convey ideas and information clearly.

Great Queens and Kings of the African Continent

POWER BUILDERS

Flag of Ethiopia (1897 – 1974)

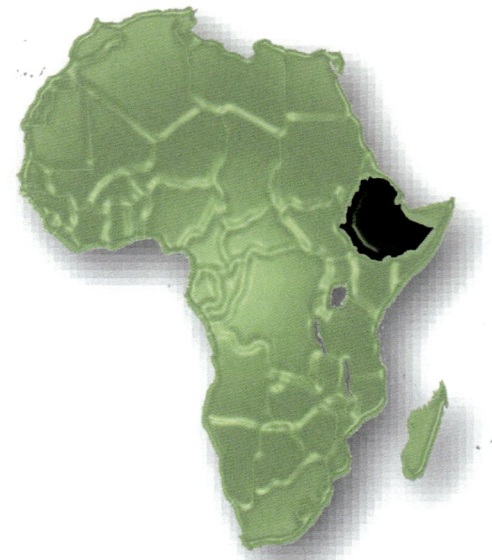

About the Images (left to right):
Emperor Menelik II of Ethiopia. The Location of Ethiopia on a map of Africa.

Pyramids of Giza in Egypt which was originally known as Kemet.

Victoria Falls

The Nile River

1. Africa is the second largest continent in the world.

2. The ancient name for Africa was Alkebulan. which means 'mother of mankind' or 'garden of Eden.'

3. 54 countries are in Africa.

4. Africa has deserts, rainforests, mountains, and savannas.

5. Africa is home to many wild animals like elephants, lions, giraffes, and zebras.

6. Ancient Kemet, known as Egypt, one of the first civilizations, in the world.

7. Africa has many different cultures with unique music, dance, and art.

8. People in Africa speak thousands of languages, including Igbo, Swahili, Arabic and French.

9. Africa has lots of natural resources like gold, diamonds, and oil.

10. Africa is home to amazing natural wonders, like the huge Sahara Desert and the beautiful Victoria Falls. It also has the Nile River, which is the longest river in the world.

Timeline of African Queens and King

Around 3000 BCE
A ruler named Narmer united Lower and Upper Kemet (ancient Egypt) and started the very first dynasty.

Around 1398 BCE
Queen Tiye becomes queen in Kemet.

Around 1478 BCE
Hatshepsut becomes the queen who ruled Kemet just like a pharaoh.

40 BCE
Queen Amanirenas becomes queen of Kush.

1312
Mansa Musa becomes king of the Mali Empire.

1624
Queen Nzinga becomes queen of the kingdom of Ndongo and Matamba in 1631.

1889
Menelik II becomes emperor of Ethiopia.

Dionysius Exiguus created the calendar that starts with the birth of Jesus Christ.

We measure time using a system that was created in Europe. This system splits history into BCE (Before Common Era) and CE (Common Era). BCE counts the years before the birth of Jesus Christ, who is the savior in Christianity, the main religion in Europe when this system was made in 525 CE. CE counts the years after Jesus was born. This way of measuring time divides history into two parts—before and after his birth.

BCE counts the years going backward from the birth of Jesus Christ. CE counts the years after his birth, starting from 1 CE, which marks the beginning of the Common Era. For example, the year 45 BCE was 45 years before his birth, while the year 1450 was 1,450 years after.

Ancient Kemet, known as **Egypt** today, was the name the people gave to their land. They called it "Kemet," which means "black land," because of the rich, dark soil along the Nile River that helped their crops grow. The Nile River was very important to them because it provided water, food, and a way to travel. The people of Kemet built incredible pyramids, temples, and statues, and their clever ideas still inspire us today.

Map of Upper and Lower Kemet

*This is a limestone head of a man, which is believed by some experts to be of King Narmer of ancient Egypt. The head is now kept at the Petrie Museum of Egyptian **Archaeology** in London.*

Narmer

Around 3000 BCE, ancient Kemet was divided into two regions: Upper Kemet and Lower Kemet. This was because of the geography of the land and how the Nile River flows. Upper Kemet was in the south, where the land was hilly and the **river valley** was narrow. Lower Kemet was in the north, where the land was flatter and the Nile **Delta** made a large, fertile area. The people in these two regions lived in different ways and had different rulers, which made them feel separate from each other.

The division happened because of the way the Nile River flows from south to north. The river helped people travel and trade, making it easier to move between the regions. Even though Upper and Lower Kemet were different, the people shared the same **culture** and language. The two regions stayed separate until a strong leader named Narmer came along. Narmer conquered Lower Kemet and brought both regions together, starting the first **dynasty** in ancient Kemet.

Directions: Please fill in the blanks with the correct answers.

1. Narmer united two regions known as <u>upper</u> and <u>lower</u> Kemet.

2. The Nile River flows from <u>south</u> to <u>north</u>.

3. Namer founded the <u>first</u> dynasty of Kemet.

Directions: Read the questions and choices carefully, and then select the best answers.

4. Why did the people call their land "Kemet"?
   A) Because it had a lot of sand
   B) Because of the rich, dark soil along the Nile River
   C) Because of the bright sunlight
   D) Because it was located in a large desert

5. Why was ancient Kemet divided into two regions?
   A) Because of the geography and how the Nile River flows
   B) Because of different weather patterns
   C) Because of different languages
   D) D) Because of different types of animals

Did you know?
Kemet is one of the oldest civilizations in the world, dating back more than 5,000 years.

Tiye of Kemet

The 18th Dynasty of Kemet was a time when Kemet was very strong and successful. It lasted from about 1550 BC to 1292 BC, and during this time, many important pharaohs ruled. One of the most famous queens of this dynasty was Queen Tiye. She was the wife of Pharaoh Amenhotep III and played a big role in Kemet's **politics** and decisions.

Pharaoh Amenhotep III

Portrait of Queen Tiye, displayed in the Egyptian Museum in Berlin, Germany.

Pharaoh Akhenaten

Tiye

Queen Tiye was an important queen of ancient Kemet who lived around 1398 BC. She was married to **Pharaoh** Amenhotep III, one of Kemet's most powerful rulers. Queen Tiye was known for her wisdom and strong leadership. Even though she was not a pharaoh, she played a key role in helping her husband rule Kemet. She was involved in making decisions about the kingdom and was well-respected by people throughout the known world.

Queen Tiye also had a big influence on her son, Akhenaten, who became pharaoh after Amenhotep III. She helped guide him in his leadership. She is remembered as a smart and powerful woman who shaped history. Her beauty, wisdom, and strength made her one of the most important queens in ancient Kemet.

Directions: Please read the questions and write the correct answers.

1. When was the 18th dynasty of Kemet founded. How many years did it last?

   1550 BCE to 1292 BCE. It lasted 258 years

2. Queen Tiye was married to which Pharoah?

   Amenhotep III

3. What was Queen Tiye's role in ancient Kemet?

   She was involved in making decisions about the kingdom.

4. Which son of Queen Tiye would become a pharaoh of Kemet?

   Akhenaten

5. What are three things Queen Tiye is remembered for?

   Beauty, wisdom, and strength

Did you know?
Queen Tiye was the grandmother to the famous pharaoh King Tut.

The Mortuary Temple of Hatshepsut is located in **Luxor, Egypt**. It was built for Queen Hatshepsut, one of Kemet's most famous female pharaohs. The temple is known for its beautiful **architecture**. It was used for religious ceremonies and to honor Hatshepsut after her death. The temple is surrounded by cliffs and is one of the most important historical sites in what is Egypt today.

Mortuary Temple of Hatshepsut in Luxor, Egypt.

Statue of Hatshepsut, displayed in The Metropolitan Museum of Art. New York City, United States

Hatshepsut

Hatshepsut was an ancient Kemetic queen who ruled as pharaoh around 3,500 years ago. She was remarkable because, unlike most rulers of her time, she was a woman. Hatshepsut became pharaoh after her husband, Thutmose II, died. She wore a fake beard and dressed like a man to show she was powerful and could rule Kemet just like any male pharaoh. Under her rule, Kemet became very wealthy from trading goods like gold and **ivory** with other countries. Hatshepsut also built many impressive temples and **monuments**, including the famous Temple of Hatshepsut.

Today, she is celebrated as one of the most powerful and successful pharaohs of ancient Kemet, known for her leadership and the monuments she built that still stand today.

Directions: Write a short response to the question below.

What were some of the achievements of Hatshepsut during her reign?

Hatshepsut was one of ancient Egypt's most successful pharaohs. She helped Egypt grow by increasing trade, building amazing temples, and making the economy stronger. Her smart decisions and strong leadership made her one of Egypt's most important rulers.

Did you know?
After the death of Hatshepsut, many of her statues and monuments were destroyed or defaced by later pharaohs, possibly because they didn't want her legacy to outshine theirs.

The Kingdom of Kush was an ancient African civilization that lived along the Nile River in region known as Nubia from about 1070 BCE to 350. It grew through trade and farming. One of the capital cities of Kush was Meroë, famous for making iron, trading with other places, and hundreds of pyramids called the Royal Cemetery of Meroë.

The Pyramids of Meroë, located in present-day Sudan.

AI generated image of Queen Amanirenas.

Statues of several Kushite rulers from the 7th century BCE in a museum in Sudan. These kings conquered Kemet and founded the 25th Dynasty.

Amanirenas

Amanirenas was a powerful queen or **Kandake**, of the Kingdom of Kush, which was located in what is now **Sudan**. She ruled over the Kingdom of Kush from around 40 BCE to 10 BCE. Amanirenas was known for her bravery and leadership skills. She led her army in battles against the **Romans** when they tried to invade her kingdom. Despite being outnumbered, she fought fiercely to protect her people and her land.

Amanirenas is also famous for her strength and determination. After a war with the Romans, she lost one of her eyes, but she did not give up. She continued to lead her people and protect her kingdom. Her courage and intelligence made her a hero in Kush, and her legacy is still celebrated today. She is remembered as a queen who loved her people and would do anything to defend her kingdom.

Directions: Please read the questions and write the correct answers.

Why do you think Amanirenas is remembered as a hero in Kush?

Amanirenas was known for her bravery and strong leadership. She led her army in battles against the Romans when they tried to take over her kingdom. She fought hard to protect her people and land.

What qualities do you think are most important for a leader to have based on Amanirenas' story?

Possible responses include – bravery, courage, and her ability to lead her people by defending them against outside danger.

Did you know?
In the Kingdom of Kush, many of the rulers were queens known as Kandakes. These queens were strong leaders who had a lot of power and made important decisions for their people. The Kandakes ruled alongside kings and often led their armies in battles, just like Amanirenas.

Mansa Musa of Mali

The **Empire** of Mali was a powerful kingdom in West Africa that flourished from the 13th to the 16th century. It became one of the richest and most important empires in the world, thanks to its control over important **trade routes**. Mali was known for its gold, salt, and other valuable resources. The empire also had great cities like Timbuktu, which was a center of learning, culture, and trade.

The remains of the University of Timbuktu, located in the country of Mali today.

Mansa Musa sitting on a throne and holding a gold coin, shown on a world map from the 1370s. CE.

Mansa Musa

Mansa Musa was the ruler of the Mali Empire in West Africa during the 14th century. He became famous for his incredible wealth, which came from the vast amounts of gold and salt in his empire. Mansa Musa's wealth was so great that when he made a **pilgrimage** to Mecca in 1324, he gave away so much gold along the way that he caused the value of gold to drop in some areas!

Mansa Musa was also a great leader who helped spread **Islam** throughout Mali and supported education and culture. He made the city of Timbuktu a major center for learning, attracting scholars, artists, and traders from all over the world. Under his rule, the Mali Empire grew stronger and his legacy continues to inspire people today.

Directions: Please fill in the blanks with the correct answers.

1. What are three facts that you learned about Mansa Musa?

   Responses can include - He was famous for his wealth, he gave away large amounts of gold, he helped spread Islam, and he helped Mali grow by building schools and mosques.

2. How did Mansa Musa impact the culture of Mali?

   Mansa Musa built schools, mosques, and libraries, making Mali an important center for learning and culture, especially in the city of Timbuktu.

Directions: Read the questions and choices carefully, and then select the best answers.

3. What made the Mali Empire one of the richest and most important empires?
   A) Control over trade routes
   B) Large population
   C) Advanced military tactics
   D) Political ties

4. Which city in Mali became famous as a center of learning, culture, and trade?
   A) Timbuktu
   B) Marrakech
   C) Cairo
   D) Lagos

5. What impact did Mansa Musa's pilgrimage to Mecca have on the value of gold?
   A) It dropped in some areas due to his generous gifts
   B) It skyrocketed across Africa
   C) It had no impact on the value of gold
   D) It caused inflation in Mali

Did you know?
Mansa Musa is often considered the wealthiest person in history. Today Mansa Musa's wealth could be around $400 billion or more.

Ndongo and Matamba were two powerful kingdoms in Africa, located in what is now **Angola**. These kingdoms were known for their strong leaders and rich cultures. Queen Nzinga of Matamba became famous for her leadership and resistance against **Portuguese colonization**. Both kingdoms played important roles in defending their land and people from outside invaders, showing bravery and strength.

This artwork shows Queen Nzinga sitting on the back of a servant during a meeting with the Portuguese. They didn't offer her a chair, only a floor mat to sit on. This was her way of standing up for herself and demanding respect, insisting on being treated equally.

Queen Njinga Mbande, also known as Queen Nzinga.

Queen Nzinga

Queen Nzinga was a strong and brave leader who ruled the Kingdoms of Ndongo and Matamba, which is in modern-day **Angola**, in the 1600s. She became queen after her brother's death and worked hard to protect her people from the Portuguese, who wanted to take control of her land. Queen Nzinga was smart and skilled in battle, and she formed **alliances** with other countries to strengthen her kingdom.

Queen Nzinga is remembered for her courage, intelligence, and ability to stand up for her people. She fought for her kingdom's freedom and was a respected leader who inspired many with her strength and determination. Her legacy continues to be a symbol of resistance and leadership for people around the world.

Directions: Write a short response to the question below.

Explain how Queen Nzinga worked hard to protect her people from injustice. What are some ways you can help protect others from unfairness or bullying?

Queen Nzinga worked hard to protect her people from injustice by standing up to powerful enemies and refusing to let them take over her land. She made smart plans to fight against the Portuguese, who wanted to take control of her kingdom.

Speak up – If I see someone being treated unfairly or bullied, or I can tell a teacher or trusted adult.

Be kind – I can stand by my friends and classmates, making sure no one feels left out or mistreated.

Set a good example – I can treat everyone with respect so others learn to do the same.

Did you know?
Queen Nzinga was not just a ruler, but also a brave warrior. She led her army in many battles against the Portuguese, using clever plans and strategies to keep her kingdom safe.

Menelik II of Ethiopia

The Empire of Ethiopia was one of the oldest and most powerful kingdoms in Africa. It lasted for many **centuries** and was known for its rich culture, traditions, and strong rulers. The empire was famous for being one of the first countries to adopt **Christianity**. It also managed to stay independent when other countries tried to take over.

A statue of Menelik II, the famous ruler of Ethiopia, in Menelik II Square, located in the capital. city of Addis Ababa.

Menelik II with his pet lion. Lions are a symbol of strength in Ethiopia, and emperors, like Menelik II, kept them as pets..

Menelik II

Menelik II was a powerful and important ruler of **Ethiopia**. He became emperor in 1889 and is best known for his role in protecting Ethiopia from being colonized. One of his most famous achievements was leading Ethiopia to victory in the Battle of **Adwa** in 1896, where his army defeated the **Italian** forces. This victory made Ethiopia one of two African countries to remain independent during the age of colonization.

In addition to his military successes, Menelik II **modernized** Ethiopia by building new roads, railways, and schools. He also helped spread Christianity throughout the country and worked to strengthen Ethiopia's **economy** and government. Menelik II's leadership has made him a beloved figure in Ethiopia's history, and his efforts to keep the country independent inspired many other African leaders.

Menelik II | Comprehension Check

Directions: Please read the questions and write the correct answers.

1. Who was Menelik II and what country did he rule?
   Menelik II was a emperor of Ethiopia.

2. How did Menelik II help protect Ethiopia from colonization?
   He lead them in battle against the Italians.

3. What famous battle did Menelik II win against the Italians? Why is it important?
   Menelik II won the Battle of Adwa in 1896. It is important because Ethiopia defeated the Italians and stayed independent.

4. Why was Menelik II's leadership important for Ethiopia?
   Menelik II modernized Ethiopia by building new roads, railways, and schools.

5. What was the impact of Menelik II's actions on the history of Africa?
   Menelik II's victory at Adwa inspired other African countries to fight for their freedom. He showed that Africans could resist European rule, making Ethiopia a symbol of strength and independence.

Did you know?
Menelik is a part of the Solomonic Dynasty, a royal family that ruled Ethiopia for many centuries, starting around the 1200s. The dynasty is said to trace its roots back to the biblical King Solomon and the Queen of Sheba.

```
  1                2
 [M][A][N][S][A][M][U][S][A]
           [Z]
           [I]
  3
 [M][E][N][E][L][I][K]
           [N]                          6
           [G]                         [K]
  4        5
 [H][A][T][S][H][E][P][S][U][T]
              [I]                      [U]
              [Y]                      [S]
                                       [H]
  7           8
 [K][E][M][E][T]
              [A]
              [L]
              [I]
```

Across

1. The famous ruler who is considered the wealthiest person in history.

3. The emperor of Ethiopia who lead his people to victory against Italy.

4. Powerful queen who ruled as a pharaoh.

7. The ancient name for Egypt.

Down

2. Powerful queen of the Kingdoms of Ndongo and Matamba

5. She was the wife of Pharaoh Amenhotep III and played an important role in Kemet's politics and decisions.

6. An ancient African civilization located along the Nile River in the region known as Nubia.

8. This empire had great cities like Timbuktu, which was a center of learning, culture, and trade.

Exploring History and Identity

Research: Choose a queen or king that interests you. Research their significance and impact on society during that time.

Record: Record a video of yourself explaining why this historical figure interests you and how does this relate to who you are today. Consider things like culture, values, and community.

Share: With permission or guidance from an adult, post on social media or a similar platform.

Tips

1. Be creative in expressing your thoughts and feelings using song or artistic expression.

2. Use historical facts to support your reflection.

Adwa: The name of a famous battle that took place in Ethiopia in 1896. It was an important moment in history because the Ethiopian army defeated the Italian army, stopping them from taking over their country.

Alliances: Agreements between countries or groups to help each other.

Angola: A country in southern Africa.

Architecture: The design and style of buildings and structures.

Centuries: A period of 100 years.

Christianity: A religion based on the teachings of Jesus Christ.

Colonization: The process of one country taking control of another area, usually for resources or land.

Map of Africa with Angola in Green

The Architecture of the Sankore Mosque (place of worship in Islam), which was part of the university of Timbuktu.

Culture: The customs, traditions, and way of life of a particular group of people.

Delta: A triangular area of land at the mouth of a river, where the river splits into several smaller parts.

Dynasty: A series of rulers from the same family.

Economy: The system of trade, money, and business that helps a country or region function.

Egypt: A country in northeastern Africa known for its ancient civilization.

Empire: A group of countries or regions controlled by one ruler or government.

Ethiopia: A country located in the Horn of Africa.

Ivory: A hard, white material from the tusks of elephants, often used to make carvings and jewelry.

Elephant Ivory Tusks

The Delta of the Nile River

Map of Africa with Egypt in Green

28

Islam: A religion based on the teachings of the prophet Muhammad, practiced by Muslims.

Italian: Relating to Italy, a country in southern Europe.

Kandake: A title used by the queens of the Kingdom of Kush.

Luxor: A city in Egypt that was once the capital of ancient Kemet, famous for its temples and monuments.

Mansa: Title given to the kings of the ancient Mali Empire.

Monuments: Large structures or statues built to honor important people or events.

Modernized: Made more up-to-date or advanced, often through technology or new ideas.

Map of Europe with Italy in Green

"The Washington Monument in Washington, D.C., also known as an obelisk, was originally designed by Africans."

Pharaoh: A ruler of ancient Kemet.

Pilgrimage: A journey to a place of religious importance.

Portuguese: Relating to Portugal, a country in southern Europe.

River valley: A low area of land next to a river, often where ancient civilizations started.

Romans: People from ancient Rome, a powerful civilization that ruled parts of Europe, Africa, and Asia.

Sudan: A country in northeastern Africa.

Trade routes: Paths or routes used for buying and selling goods between different places.

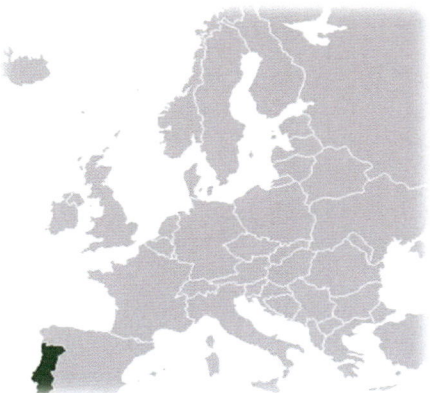

Map of Europe with Portugal in Green

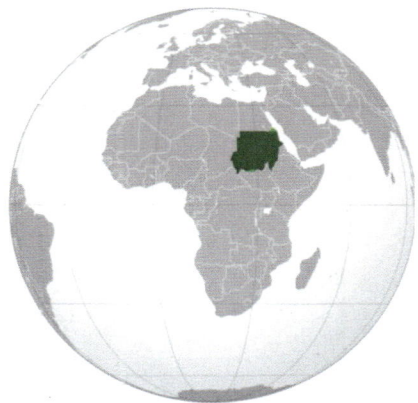

Map of Africa with Sudan in Green

Supplemental Resources – Graphic Organizers and Slide Deck

The Great Queens and Kings of the African Continent - Central Idea

Student Workbook pages 9 – 21

Activity 2: Making Connections – Planner

Student Workbook page 4

Blank Map of Africa

Slide Deck and Printable Graphic Organizers

The Great Queens and Kings
of the African Continent
Central Idea

Central Idea:

Details:

Details:

Details:

Summary :

Activity 2: Making Connections

Research Notes:

Script:

_____

_____

_____

_____

_____

_____

_____

_____

_____

Africa

Slide Deck
https://boldly.black/slidedeck2

Printable Graphic Organizers
https://boldly.black/graphic45

Password (Case Sensitive)
TeachAfrica2

References

BlackPast. *BlackPast*. Accessed January 2, 2025. https://www.blackpast.org

Center for African Studies, Howard University. The Gold Road. Accessed December 2, 2024. https://cfas.howard.edu/outreach/gold-road.

Gates, Henry Louis, Jr. 2017. Africa's Great Civilizations. Directed by Henry Louis Gates Jr. Arlington, VA: PBS

Parker, John. Great Kingdoms of Africa. Berkeley: University of California Press, 2023.

Williams, Chancellor. 1987. Destruction of Black Civilization: Great Issues of a Race from 4500 B.C. to 2000 A.D. Third World Press.

"Until the lions have their historians, tales of the hunt shall always glorify the hunter."

African Proverb

Made in the USA
Monee, IL
07 March 2025

13627931R00024